D1384460

WAY GROSS SCIENCE™

5/2019
STRAND PRICE
$ 2.00

THE GROSS SCIENCE OF
SNEEZING, COUGHING, AND VOMITING

RACHEL GLUCKSTERN

rosen publishing's
rosen central®

New York

Published in 2019 by The Rosen Publishing Group, Inc.
29 East 21st Street, New York, NY 10010

Library of Congress Cataloging-in-Publication Data

Names: Gluckstern, Rachel, author.
Title: The gross science of sneezing, coughing, and vomiting / Rachel Gluckstern.
Description: New York : Rosen Central, 2019. | Series: Way gross science | Audience: Grades 5–8. | Includes bibliographical references and index.
Identifiers: LCCN 2017050377| ISBN 9781508181743 (library bound) | ISBN 9781508181750 (paperback)
Subjects: LCSH: Sneezing—Juvenile literature. | Cough—Juvenile literature. | Vomiting—Juvenile literature.
Classification: LCC QP123.8 .G58 2019 | DDC 612.2—dc23

LC record available at https://lccn.loc.gov/2017050377

Manufactured in the United States of America

CONTENTS

INTRODUCTION

Picture it: a serious math test is in progress, but you can't focus on it. Something's building up inside you, a powerful urge your body can't fight down. Maybe your nose is tingling. Maybe your throat is itchy. Maybe your stomach is hurting and twitching. You can feel the unpleasant sensation rising up through your chest, your throat, maybe up your nose! Whatever's about to happen, you know it's going to be loud and potentially super gross. This could be the most embarrassing moment *ever*. Why does the body have to do something so icky? What possible good can come out of sneezing, coughing, or vomiting?

Well, a lot of good, actually. The reaction or reflex that causes a person to sneeze, cough, or throw up means that something is wrong inside one's body, and the reflex happens when the body is trying to protect itself. It's cleaning up and throwing out any unwanted visitors. We think of sneezing, coughing, or vomiting as symptoms of being sick. However, often, these reflexes kick in to repel a change in the physical environment, such as a nonsmoker being around people using tobacco products. The reflexes might even work together in some cases—a person entering a very dusty room is sure to sneeze, thanks to all the irritating particles floating around, but enough inhalations of the dust, and the internal buildup will produce a coughing fit, too.

Every part of the body has a purpose, and what may seem totally disgusting can actually be very helpful to one's overall health. The amount of snot produced by sneezing or its color can provide a valuable insight into what's causing that particular symptom. The difference between a dry cough and a wet one—which can be expelling a lot of harmful germs—is crucial to understand.

Although they're uncomfortable, sneezing, coughing, and vomiting can be very helpful reactions. But you don't have to be sick in order to sneeze, cough, or throw up.

The connection, too, between the respiratory system and the gastro-intestinal tract is important to understand. Perhaps sneezing alone isn't a sign of anything serious. But if too much snot is being produced, the post-nasal drip can irritate the throat enough to start some serious coughing, especially when you're lying down. Acid reflux can have an effect on the color of the mucus, and enough coughing can trigger a bout of nausea that starts bringing up the bile. That bile is so acidic, it can really damage the tissues of the respiratory system, which leads to affecting the production of mucus. What might seem like an isolated symptom can lead to a whole chain reaction throughout the body. It's almost like a traffic jam! Ultimately the body will benefit from ridding itself of outside bacteria, physical particles, or ingested irritants. The process, however, can be painful. It can be embarrassing. It can be very, *very* gross. But there's a science behind all the tough times of nose-blowing, cough syrup–induced bedtimes and days of eating only saltines and drinking ginger ale. And it's fascinating! And also gross.

CHAPTER ONE

SNEEZING

There's a tingling in your nose. It's itching, and rubbing it just makes it worse. In fact, a lot of pressure is building up behind your face! Oh no, what's happening?

The process of sneezing is the same whether it's a buildup of germs or a buildup of physical foreign objects in your respiratory system. Eventually, your body wants to get rid of the irritants. But do you even know what's getting irritated in your body? By learning about what the respiratory system does, it will make more sense as to why your body would need to sneeze at some point.

WHY DO I SNEEZE?

The nose is crucial in providing a pathway for the essential oxygen in the air. However, with every breath in, dust and other foreign particles—including germs—are being inhaled, too. Inside, the nasal passages are lined with nose hairs, which do more than just look unattractive. These hairs are known as the cilia. They act as filters, trying to keep the contaminants from reaching the more sensitive areas of the respiratory system.

Meanwhile, you don't even have to be sneezing to be producing snot! The human body produces over a quart (a little bit under a liter) of snot every day! WebMD compares mucus to the "oil in the engine.

Mucus may be gross, but it's essential to help keep the body's machinery running smoothly. It's the "oil" that coats the engine of your respiratory system.

Without [it], the engine seizes." Snot coats all the delicate internal areas of the body, including the "mouth, nose, sinuses, throat, lungs, and gastrointestinal tract." This protective lining ensures that the tissues don't dry out. If the cilia are the filters, the mucus is the "flypaper," catching bacteria, virus germs, and dust particles before they advance deeper into the body.

Eventually the irritants build up too much in the upper respiratory system for the body to tolerate their presence any longer. Ever notice that you take a deep breath in before you sneeze? That inhalation triggers the flap at the back of throat—known as the epiglottis—to close up. All the muscles in the chest begin tightening. As a result, there's so much pressure on the air in the lungs that it will have to explode out at tremendous speed. How fast? If the sneeze is powerful enough, it can be as fast as 525 feet (160 meters) per second!

The act of sneezing is powerful. A big sneeze can be so forceful that it's hard to believe your head stays intact afterward!

According to *Magill's Medical Guide*, the air and neighboring mucus comes out the nose instead of the mouth, thanks to the contraction of the pharynx muscles, which are the throat's muscles. The tongue presses against the roof of the mouth, which helps seal up the mouth and keeps the air pushing up and out the nasal passages.

GERM WARFARE OR BAD ENVIRONMENT?

Sneezing isn't always a sign of being sick. It's easy to connect it with a cold or the flu. But allergies are generally not caused by viruses or contagious bacteria, so sometimes—often—a sneeze is the reflex triggered by the environment around a person instead. It's how one sneezes, and what one produces, that can be the real test of whether or not a sneeze

SNOT COLOR WARNING CHART

According to Business Insider, the color of mucus can give an indication of what's wrong with the body. Don't take it as an official diagnosis, but do pay attention to it and let a doctor know when it seems appropriate for you to talk to one:

CLEAR	Clear mucus is generally a good sign that everything's in good working order.	Excessive amounts indicate allergy or cold.
WHITE	High probability that the nasal passages are swollen, which lessens the mucus flow and dries it out.	Infection or cold are possible. Could also be allergies, dairy, food/drink that dehydrates a person, like coffee or tea, or it might be acid reflux.
YELLOW	The body is starting to fight an infection, probably a cold.	The color is caused by dead white blood cells, which tried to destroy the infectious particles.
GREEN	If accompanied by fever and nausea, call a doctor. If it's still green after twelve days, it may be a sinus infection.	The immune system is sacrificing lots of white blood cells to fight off infection.
PINK/ RED	The nasal passages themselves have become dry and irritated.	There may be blood in the mucus as a result of blowing your nose too hard or too often.

BROWN	Too much exposure to fire, heavy dust, or smoking tobacco products can produce brown mucus. Coughing up brown snot may indicate bronchitis.	Color suggests dried blood in nasal passages.
BLACK	If accompanied by fever, chills, and difficulty breathing, this color may indicate a fungal infection.	If no other symptoms are present, black snot can be a result of high exposure to a dangerous environment that's full of foreign particles, like smoke or a very dusty construction site.

means a cold or flu—or possibly something even more serious (which happens way, way less often).

When trying to determine whether it's a disease or environmental, checking to see if you have any other symptoms is very helpful. A fever, exhaustion, sore throat, sinus pressure, or a cough are all common signs of possible illness when they accompany sneezing. However, allergies are marked more by burning eyes and heavy sneezing, but not necessarily coughing or swollen lymph nodes.

An allergy attack and a cold can both involve running noses, so it's important to consider whether the consistency of the mucus being expelled has changed. Although some people just have naturally thick and sticky snot all the time, a change in consistency can indicate a change in the body, too. An overproduction of mucus can also be caused by allergies or disease, a reaction to spicy food, or even be a reaction to dairy, which is known as gustatory rhinitis.

If there is the concern that a sneeze is the sign of disease, and that the infection is spreading, try to see if anything is being expelled as you sneeze. Air and dry sneezing are probably allergies or caused by the surrounding environment. A visible "cloud" made up of mucus droplets is really what carries lots of contagious germs. Chances of infection increase in warm, poorly ventilated areas, especially ones with lots of people.

OTHER WAYS TO LOSE YOUR HEAD

Outside of a cold or a spicy taco, there are other triggers for sneezing. Some of them sound crazy! Bright lights can trigger such a reaction

Spicy food stimulates your sneezing reflex, but a big sneeze can feel really good when you're congested. And sometimes, the sneeze risk is worth a tasty taco.

according to *Popular Science*. This is known as a photic sneeze, and about 25 percent of the world's population is affected by the sun or very bright lights. When the optic nerves of these people are overwhelmed with light, they sneeze. It's possible that having allergies can make one more sensitive, or that the light "stimulates facial nerves" enough to make it happen.

A letter to the *International Journal of Urology*—that's the science of pee if you want to eventually study gross science full time—says that sneezing after a large meal is very common. It's known as the Achoo syndrome. The letter went on to note the case study of an older man who found himself sneezing whenever his bladder was full. These reactions aren't necessarily linked to any diseases, but what triggers a sneeze may be more unexpected than a cold.

CHAPTER TWO

COUGHING

The single most common reason someone visits the doctor is regarding a cough. It can be dry. It can be accompanied by mucus or "sputum." It can last for days or weeks or be gone as quickly as it came. Regardless, that itchy feeling in the back of the throat and pressure in the lungs are combining into something really uncomfortable.

HOW IT WORKS AGAINST YOU

Coughing is a protective reflex working to expel foreign particles and sputum from the airways, especially in the lungs. *Magill's Medical Guide* details the process as beginning with the reflex stimulating the nerves of the larynx, the trachea or the windpipe, and the bronchial tubes. Then the pressure increases in the chest, thanks to the tightening of the muscles there and in the diaphragm. This pressure is increased by the glottis closing up, which is the entry to the windpipe being blocked off. Finally, the glottis bursts open again to allow the trapped air to rush out the mouth. Hopefully, it will bring any foreign particles along with it to help clear out the airways.

As unpleasant as the experience can be, an article from *Harvard Health Publishing* points out that coughing is a strong weapon in the body's arsenal for defense against disease. "Coughing expels mucus,

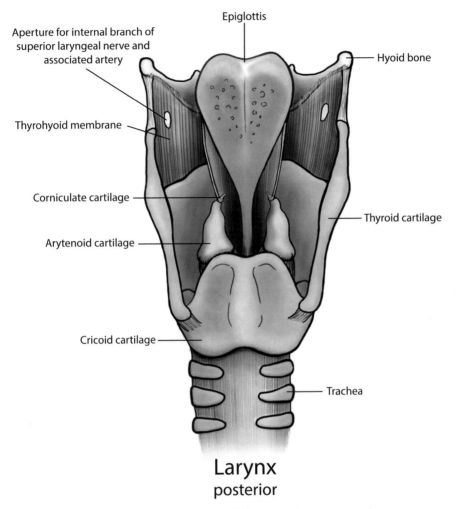

Epiglottis

Aperture for internal branch of
superior laryngeal nerve and
associated artery

Hyoid bone

Thyrohyoid membrane

Corniculate cartilage

Thyroid cartilage

Arytenoid cartilage

Cricoid cartilage

Trachea

Larynx
posterior

The larynx is a complicated part of your respiratory system. A cough has to travel a long way from your lungs to leave through your mouth.

microbes, and foreign particles from the respiratory tract, protecting the lungs from infection and inflammatories." A cough may hurt, but it's actually being super helpful by keeping the lungs clear and the airways flowing. Still, it can be very uncomfortable to cough, especially strongly.

The reflexes that cause coughing can force the air out practically at the speed of sound, which is why it creates the "barking" noise.

BUT WHAT'S WRONG WITH YOU?

According to the health guide supplied by the *New York Times*, a cough can be acute, subacute, or chronic. Acute coughs are the most common and tend to accompany a cold, flu, or sinus infection. They descend on the body quickly and are gone again within three weeks. A subacute cough will leave eventually, but it will last three to eight weeks, and it generally indicates something more serious, like pneumonia or bronchitis. These types of infections generally require a trip to the doctor and medications.

A chronic cough indicates an ongoing condition like asthma or GERD (gastroesophageal reflux disease), which seems surprising. In extreme

WHAT IS WHOOPING COUGH?

Whooping cough is a serious respiratory infection caused by the bacteria *Bordetella pertussis*. It causes such a powerful, uncontrollable cough that breathing can become very difficult. This makes it especially dangerous for babies and small children who catch the disease.

At one point, whooping cough ravaged the United States, causing approximately nine thousand deaths per year. Thanks to vaccines, that number has dropped dramatically to fewer than thirty deaths a year.

The condition gets its name from the sound that a patient makes when trying to breathe after a bout of serious coughing.

cases, a chronic cough can be the sign of something very serious, although mainly that's a concern for smokers, who will have lingering coughs and "benign" conditions—which can, of course, develop into something far more serious if they don't stop smoking.

Germs use coughing to spread themselves to new hosts. Seeing if other symptoms are present can help determine if the cough is medical or environmental—or a side effect of a different condition altogether.

WET OR DRY?

What kind of cough you have may help to determine what's causing it. A wet cough is a "productive" cough because it brings physical stuff up with it, like sputum, the mucus that collects in the lungs. This is an effort done by the body to try and clear itself out of harmful particles. Postnasal drip, also known as the upper airway cough syndrome, is a result of overproduction of mucus. When the snot slides down the throat, it tickles the surrounding nerves and triggers the coughing reaction. Such dripping tends to be the result of allergies, airborne particles like dust or chemicals, sinus issues, and some viruses. Postnasal drip is especially annoying at night when one is trying to sleep. At that time, it mainly pools in the upper trachea, triggering a cough far more easily.

A dry cough can indicate something more chronic or more environmental. It might be the flu; it might be from asthma or pneumonia. It might also be a dry, dusty environment causing the tickling at the back of the throat. A dry cough is "unproductive," in that it won't bring anything up—although it probably can feel unproductive as in "useless" as well. A chronic cough is usually thought of as "hypersensitive." It affects about 12 percent of the general population in some form or another.

Another study revealed that children coughing due to colds were a static percentage of children affected by disease, which means the number of children who cough when they get sick doesn't vary much at all.

Children who coughed because of exercise, dust, or allergens became more likely to be triggered by those same influences more often as they get older. In other words, maybe we won't become more vulnerable to disease as we grow up, but we can and probably will become more sensitive to our surroundings.

One chronic condition to be especially mindful of is asthma. Although we typically think of the symptoms as being short of breath and wheezing, some patients only cough. A person suffering from an asthmatic chronic cough condition will only cough as a symptom. It can be quite

Congestion in your chest can be a cause of a wet cough, which is also known as a productive cough.

frequent, especially at night. This is known as cough-variant asthma. Like other forms of asthma, it can be triggered by allergens, dust, or cold air.

Other forms of asthma might lean more toward productive coughing, with overproduction of snot being a classic symptom. As with acute coughing, pay attention to any other symptoms, such as fever. They can help you determine whether you might want to see a doctor—or whether you just need to vacuum your room.

CHAPTER THREE

VOMITING

There's not much worse than vomiting, let's be honest. The feeling of dread accompanying the rising nausea is as scary as any horror movie you might've seen recently—and probably a few that you haven't. It's painful when it's happening, and when you're done, you're exhausted. You've lost food, fluids, dignity—but hopefully you've also eliminated some pretty fierce toxins from your body.

HOW DO I VOMIT?

Throwing up goes beyond the mere physical reflex your body might do against other invaders. Vomiting, also known as emesis, is actually caused by a signal in your brain. There are two brain centers that control emesis, and they're both located in the medulla oblongata, which regulates the motor functions of the body, like eating. One of these centers is called the vomiting center, which is the main driver in signaling the body to forcefully eject the contents of one's stomach thought the mouth. Although the feeling of nausea often warns the patient of impending emesis, one can throw up without feeling nauseated first, but that will be mainly due to influences like extreme physical exertion.

Nausea can be a warning sign of impending emesis, which is the act of vomiting. However, just feeling nauseated doesn't automatically mean you're going to throw up.

When the vomiting center is triggered, the smooth muscles that line the digestive tract begin to contract. They start at the small intestine and move up through the stomach and throat until the contents are expelled. The triggers of the vomiting center tend to be due to other parts of the body being stressed or diseased. However, the chemoreceptor trigger is tripped by toxins and chemicals if you ingest something very bad for you, like too much aspirin or another medication accidentally. Once the chemoreceptor is triggered, it activates the vomiting center, and the same process initiates.

WHY DO I VOMIT?

It's easy to think of vomiting as being the result of something like the stomach flu or a bad meal. In other words, throwing up seems to be

THE THREE STAGES OF VOMITING

According to *Magill's Medical Guide*, the act of throwing up can be divided into three stages:

PREEJECTION: This is when the nausea kicks in, the mouth fills with excess saliva, and the heart starts beating faster.

EJECTION: The actual act of vomiting, which may be emesis as described, or retching, which is considered nonproductive emesis or dry heaving.

POSTEJECTION: The body is exhausted and shuts down. The feeling of nausea is temporarily relieved. Often, the body only needs to purge itself once and then rest to heal up.

most connected to the stomach. However, studies show that many causes are often due to diseases outside the gastrointestinal tract. Something like a stone in the bile duct can send a signal to the vomiting center. Or perhaps a signal can come from the bloodstream, which is why it's very important to be sure to pay attention to warning labels on medication and only take the recommended dosages.

Because there can be so many different ways to trip the vomiting center's trigger, it's important to pay attention to what's coming up if anything even does. Projectile vomiting is caused by gastric outlet obstruction, which generally means ingesting something you shouldn't have. Regurgitation is similar to clinical emesis, but it may be more passive and the contents will come from the esophagus rather than the stomach. Yellow vomit is a sign of bile, which is the acid in the stomach that helps digestion, especially with fatty foods. This kind of vomiting will generally

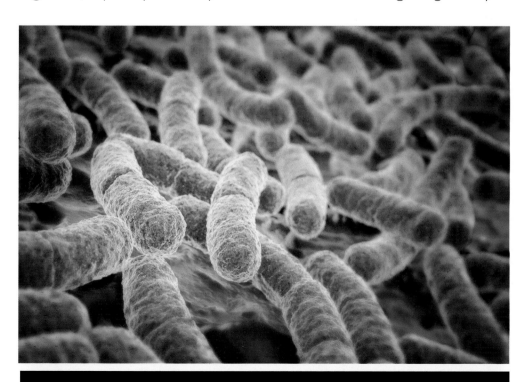

E. coli food poisoning can cause severe diarrhea and vomiting. It is the cause of thousands of hospitalizations in the United States each year.

happen after a meal. Green vomit is a sign of even more bile, indicating that a bowel may be blocked by hernia or gallstones.

Vomiting blood is clearly a sign of something being wrong, like a cut to the esophagus and stomach. At times, the bile congeals with blood, and the vomit will look like coffee grounds when it comes up. It can be a sign that the liver is in distress or possibly acid reflex is getting very damaging. There may even be an ulcer. These conditions aren't very common, especially for kids and teens, so don't be surprised if you never experience such symptoms. It's just good to be informed.

IF I'M NOT SICK, WHAT'S GOING ON?

One of the biggest reasons one throws up is due to motion sickness. That's all due to an outside influence and nothing to do with germs at all. Motion sickness is considered to be the conflict between sensory inputs. In other words, when you're in motion while also focusing on something else, this can put a lot of stress on the mind and can trigger the vomiting center signals. Reading while in a car might be an example of this conflict, especially on a bumpy road. It's not absolutely always going to happen— different people have different reactions—but the more stress that being in motion causes, the more likely it is you might throw up.

It might not even be forewarned with the feeling of nausea. Sometimes, the trigger is tripped without any signs beforehand at all. Not wanting to split up focus is probably why people like to say, "Sit back and enjoy the ride!" Paying attention only to the experience of the motion may lessen the chances of being negatively affected by the movement.

Related to motion sickness is overexertion—doing too much effort in bad conditions. Maybe it's working outdoors in hot sunlight. Maybe it's running or cycling too long without rest breaks and especially without water breaks. *Runner's World* details the way people can run a race

incorrectly, causing them to throw up afterward. It's not considered a sign that one really pushed oneself and had a good workout. Instead, it's considered running a race the wrong way. A runner should finish up feeling good about the workout. Sure, runners might feel exhausted, ready to collapse, and wanting a nap and a gallon of water, but they should also feel happy, accomplished, and full of the euphoria that comes with working out correctly.

The biggest possible cause of vomiting after overexertion is dehydration. Not enough water makes a body more likely to trigger that vomiting

Don't buy into the harmful myth of "no pain, no gain." Keep yourself hydrated and don't overexert yourself when running or exercising in general.

center. Sweating heavily due to high-impact exercise or labors can dry a body out quickly. *Runner's World* notes that losing more than 4 percent of one's body weight after a run can mean that the gut isn't absorbing liquids correctly anymore, leading to nausea. The *New York Times Health Guide* recommends maintaining hydration with sipping "frequent, small amounts of clear liquid." Small kids are often recommended to drink something like Pedialyte, which helps manage fluid absorption. Whatever else might be affecting you, drinking something may be the biggest help of all.

CHAPTER FOUR

EVERYTHING OUT NOW!

The human body is weird. It might seem like sneezing, coughing, and vomiting are separate reactions, or that they're three levels for germs and irritants to clear, like in a puzzle platform video game. However, there can be surprising connections between the three reflexes. It's why even though the cough is the most common reason people go see a doctor, the presence of heavy sneezing, a change in mucus production, or nausea and vomiting accompanying the cough can help a doctor figure out what's wrong much more accurately. The snot that's expelled when vomiting sometimes can mean something specific as to what's triggering the vomiting center in the brain. And the flow of mucus down the throat can be a big part of the reason your cough is still going strong!

SNOT IN MY LUNGS!

Of course, when we start getting sick, we worry that it's not just going to be a mild infection, like a cold. Maybe it's the flu, which can be more severe than a cold, even deadly. That's why we get flu shots each year (or should). Colds and flus are both respiratory diseases, according to the Centers for Disease Control and Prevention (CDC), but they're caused by different viruses. However, the CDC also mentions that "people with

colds are more likely to have a runny or stuffy nose." The fever, chills, muscle and body aches, headache, and fatigue one can have are all signs of the flu. A cold will generally have fewer symptoms or feel less severe.

Snot gathering in the chest and lungs can be a problem with severe infections, like bronchitis, although they can also be a reaction to the outside environment. Whether it's an infection caused by disease, or an infection caused by a condition such as asthma, white blood cells are the first line of defense against the damage that ingesting irritants can do to a body. People suffering from asthma can experience a hyperreactive response, which makes the lungs close up very suddenly and completely when inhaling particles. Then when people try to relax and breathe out again, the constriction can be too strong to overcome right away.

Getting an annual flu shot is a good way to avoid spending a lot of time coughing, sneezing, and possibly vomiting! And by getting one, you help keep your community healthy, too.

The hyperreactive stage can then be followed by the inflammatory response, which is when the white blood cells step in. Their defense will cause the breathing passages to "swell, to fill with fluid, and to produce a thick sticky mucus." That snot is also known as phlegm, which is a lot of fun to say, although it's not fun to experience it. Bronchitis is also an inflammation, which is presumably why it also will produce the thick snot caused by dead white blood cells. However, this is a disease that usually grows out of a cold, not a symptom or response as part of an ongoing condition. Asthma can't spread like an infection can.

LET IT ALL OUT!

Ever coughed so hard, you threw up? It happens! Generally, though, it's only when symptoms like coughing up blood, trouble breathing, dehydration, or blue face, tongue, or lips are present that it becomes a true emergency. Mainly it just takes a cough hard enough to stress the body out and trigger the vomiting center. Asthma, particularly the form known as cough-variant asthma, in which the only symptom is coughing, can be strong enough to make the body vomit.

Postnasal drip, which is caused by mucus sliding down the throat, can also make someone throw up, tying all three together! Acute bronchitis and pneumonia are both instances of when the body will experience power productive coughing, which means the cough is forcing out something physical—usually snot—out of the patient. Bronchitis can also be severe enough to leave patients with a dry

Asthma affects far more people than we know in far more ways than we assume. One symptom is intense coughing!

WHAT IS GERD?

Out of all the factors that can cause sneezing, coughing, or vomiting, GERD is the most likely to cause all three at the same time. GERD is the short way of saying gastroesophageal reflex disease. It's not acid reflux, although both can occur in the lower esophagus. GERD is also known as the cause of heartburn, and it's been linked with asthma. The *New York Times Health Guide* estimates that at least half of asthma patients also have GERD, although the relationship between them is unclear. Which causes which?

GERD occurs when the contents of the stomach are flowing up into the esophagus. Common symptoms include burping, a sour taste in the mouth, and bad breath in addition to heartburn. However, instead of heartburn, the acid can trigger the cough reflex instead.

wheezing cough that can stick with them even after the disease itself is gone. This cough can still trigger a reaction of vomiting.

A BOWL AND A KLEENEX

Sometimes, when people throw up, they eject a lot of mucus, too, especially out through the nose. Sometimes, that can just mean the need to vomit was so strong, the physical reaction was powerful enough to drive everything out of your body. Other times, it may be associated with specific infections.

WebMD lists the most common causes of vomiting and the presence of thick sticky mucus as being food poisoning; diabetic ketoacidosis, which is a complication of diabetes when the body is creating large amounts of

The most common cause of vomiting is motion sickness, not disease. When there's too much stress on your body, sometimes your brain can react only by making you throw up.

blood acids; and constipation. The last is especially true for children, so pay attention to how often you poop!

Like other triggers for the act of vomiting itself, the addition of the mucus can also be a sign of anxiety, dehydration, lactose intolerance, or motion sickness. There are plenty of reasons why we throw up, unfortunately, but out of all the symptoms to watch out for, vomiting is the one most associated with noninfectious concerns, so it's not always the sign of any bad disease.

MYTHS AND FACTS

Myth: If you don't close your eyes when you sneeze, they'll pop right out of your head!

Fact: According to Laura Gehl, also known as "Dr. Cy Borg," for *Odyssey*, your eyes automatically close as part of the sneezing reflex. However, it's possible to fight against that reaction—but it takes a lot of effort, and all you might get is snot in your eyes from your sneeze.

Myth: Asthma is always accompanied by a wheezing cough.

Fact: Asthma expresses itself in many ways. One form is known as cough-variant asthma, and the only symptom of its presence is a chronic cough.

Myth: Sometimes, people can vomit so hard, they throw up feces (poop)!

Fact: This is extremely unlikely to happen—but not impossible. It's due to a very abnormal issue with your guts, where the lining of the intestines are leaking and the contents within are mixing when they shouldn't. Something has to go very, very wrong for this to happen, so alert a doctor right away if it does.

CHAPTER FIVE

TAKE CARE AND RUN FOR COVER!

Whether you're sneezing, coughing, or vomiting, often the best treatment is some rest and fluids. Medications can soothe these conditions when they're specific symptoms of specific diseases, but there's no cure-all quick-fix. So be kind to your body and treat it with care when you are sick. And also try to avoid spreading it to others.

SELF-CARE

There are many home treatments that can ease the discomfort of sneezing, coughing, or vomiting. Some involve lying still and staying hydrated. Some might be a little more involved, so be sure you've discussed them with a doctor and parent or guardian first.

For example, if you're trying to determine whether a constant cough is being caused by postnasal drip or not, doing something to drain out the nasal passages is one kind of treatment. Inhaling steam from a shower or a teakettle or using saline nose spray can help clear them. But those are steps that need consultation with an adult first. However, if

Be sure to treat your illnesses and conditions with lots of fluids and light, soft foods. Being kind to your stomach is being kind to yourself.

the cough doesn't stop after such irrigations, postnasal drip is probably not the cause, which can be useful for you and your doctor to know.

It's also best to let yourself cough as much as possible if you can stand it. That's how the body is cleaning itself of infectious particles and irritants. There's no medication that can shorten the amount of time spent suffering from an acute or subacute cough, but there are treatments to ease your throat, like honey in hot water or tea. An expectorant can thin out the mucus that's clogging the airways in order to drain them out faster. Cough suppressants and syrups should really be confined to bedtimes, to help you sleep.

When it comes to nausea, that queasy feeling is letting you know there's danger of vomiting, but it's not certain yet that you're going to throw up. WebMD recommends sitting still or lying in a propped-up position. This can reduce the chances of the nausea getting stronger. If you eat, eat small meals, and eat them slowly. Avoid anything that might be too rich, spicy, or high in fiber. Drinking clear liquids in small amounts can also help when feeling nauseated, especially in between meals, not during them.

It's very important to stay somewhat upright when you're worried about throwing up. Don't lie on your back. Instead, keep your head elevated about a foot above your stomach. If you need to throw up, and you're on your back, you're in danger of choking on the vomit because the gag reflex can't stay intact. The gag reflex keeps the vomit from entering your respiratory system, like your lungs. So do what you can to sit up if it seems like you're going to throw up. Keep a lined trashcan or bucket nearby in case of emergencies.

IS MY FACE RED?

It's *so* embarrassing to make any kind of scene in public. Sometimes, it feels like the more you're trying to prevent the reflex, the more powerful it is when it happens. Throwing up in public is the worst. Everyone looks really grossed out, and you can't pretend like nothing happened. Here's what you should keep in mind:

Better out than in: Yes, the timing is inconvenient, but when the body is trying to expel or eject contents and irritants, it's because there are things inside that can cause harm if they stay there. So no matter when it happens, know that it happened for a good reason.

Excuse yourself: If you're all anxious that you're causing too much noise and that everyone is looking at you, it's fine to take yourself elsewhere and finish the coughing or sneezing attack more comfortably. Since nausea often warns a person when she or he is in danger of puking, that can be an excellent time to leave a public area or classroom before the vomiting center is triggered.

No matter where you are, it's always okay to get help or just excuse yourself if you're feeling sick. Don't sit and hope it'll pass. Take care of yourself!

HOW TO GREET A SNEEZE

It's common to say, "Bless you" after a sneeze, but has that always been true? According to Dr. Aronson, sneezing has shown up in ancient Greek documents and was often considered a sign of having good fortune. Romans would "greet" sneezing, which once led the statesman Pliny to say, "Why greet sneezing?" (Except he said it in Latin.)

Some cultures still consider sneezing a good omen, just like the Greeks might have done, and so they respond to sneezes with *santé*, which means "health" in French, *gesundheit*, which is "health" in German, or *morgen mooi weer*, which is Dutch for "nice weather tomorrow." Other cultures consider sneezing as something in need of good fortune. So their greetings are like "Bless you," such as "May you live long" or *Tapā'īṁ lāmō jīvana bitā'aunuhuncha* in Nepali, "a fortunate occurrence" or *xìngyùn de shì* in Chinese, or the Irish, who say, *féadfaidh sé dul ceart*, which can mean, "may it go right."

Be kind to yourself and others: It's easy to be grossed out when someone coughs up a lot of phlegm, sneezes all over the math test, or throws up. And there will always be mean people who will find it funny. But it's actually a common occurrence that even adults have to deal with at times, so don't let yourself dwell on it too much. Just say to yourself, "I was sick, and it had to come out, and that's okay." At some point, you may see someone else suffer the same condition in public, and they'll be embarrassed, too. Feel free to offer help if they need any at that time, like offering a tissue, calling a parent, or just letting them know you've been sick in public, too.

BE SMART, DON'T SHARE

Although sneezing, coughing, and vomiting happen for many reasons other than germs, it's always best to treat these occurrences like they might be contagious. That way, you can help prevent the spreading of disease or causing some other kind of infection.

Wash your hands frequently after eating, after sneezing or coughing, after using the bathroom, and after handling anything that might carry germs.

Cough or sneeze into a tissue or sleeve and always keep the mouth covered when you do.

Be prepared. Having a cough drop and tissues with you at all times can be very helpful for you or someone else needing assistance.

Rest and stay away from people when you feel sick. Never be afraid to ask someone for help.

Practicing good hygiene is an easy way to greatly reduce the spread of infectious or irritating particles. Always wash your hands before and after eating or cooking and after going to the bathroom.

10 GREAT QUESTIONS TO ASK
A DOCTOR

1. Why am I coughing more at night?
2. What does the color of my mucus mean?
3. What's the difference between a cold and the flu?
4. Can I have seasonal allergies and still get sick?
5. I didn't feel any nausea, so why did I throw up?
6. If I have asthma, what are the ways we can treat it?
7. I felt sick after taking a certain kind of medication. Did I take too much?
8. How can I prevent motion sickness?
9. What's the best way to stay hydrated?
10. How long should I deal with multiple symptoms before seeing a doctor?

GLOSSARY

asthma A physical condition that causes difficulty breathing.

bile Acid in the stomach that helps digest food.

chemoreceptor zone The area in the brain that triggers the vomiting center when affected by toxins or drugs.

chronic A constant condition that doesn't go away.

cilia The hairs in the nose that filter foreign particles.

emesis Vomiting.

esophagus The passageway that connects the mouth to the stomach through the throat.

GERD Gastroesophageal disease, the primary cause of heartburn.

intestines Your guts; long tubes that help digest the food after it leaves the stomach and absorb nutrients into the bloodstream.

medulla oblongata The part of the brain that controls the motor functions.

mucus The sticky liquid that covers the soft tissues of the respiratory system to keep them from drying out.

pharynx The juncture of the nasal passages to the mouth and throat.

postnasal drip Mucus that's slid down the throat and irritated the nerves there.

productive cough A cough that produces fluids like sputum.

regurgitation A condition similar to vomiting; however, it brings up contents from the esophagus, not the stomach.

retching Nonproductive vomiting, or dry heaving.

sputum The thick mucus that clogs your lungs when you're sick.

trachea The tube that carries air in and out of your neck and lungs.

vomiting center The area of the brain that signals the body to vomit.

FOR MORE INFORMATION

Canadian Paediatric Society
2305 St. Laurent Boulevard, Suite 100
Ottawa, ON K1G 4J8
(613) 526-9397
Website: http://www.caringforkids.cps.ca
Facebook: @caring for kids.cps.ca
Twitter: @CaringforKids
This website offers useful information for parents by Canada's
    pediatricians.

Center for Young Women's Health
333 Longwood Avenue, 5th Floor
Boston, MA 02115
(617) 355-2994
Website: https://youngwomenshealth.org
Twitter: @CYWH
This site is a partnership associated with Boston's Children's Hospital,
    designed to promote knowledge and advice for young women in
    need of resources on their health.

Centers for Disease Control and Prevention
1600 Clifton Road
Atlanta, GA 30329-4027
(800) 232-4636
Website: https://www.cdc.gov/nchs/fastats/child-health.htm
Facebook: @CDC
Twitter: @CDCgov
Instagram: @cdcgov
This is a quick resource from the Centers for Disease Control and
    Prevention to check your health and monitor it.

Northwestern's Children's Practice
680 North Lake Shore Drive, Suite 1050
Chicago, IL 60611
(312) 642-5515
Website: http://www.nwcppediatrics.com/contents/is-my-child-sick
Facebook: @NWCP123
This website is for the Northwestern's Children's Practice. Although the
pediatricians are located in Chicago, the site is full of advice for everyone.

WebMD
WebMD LLC
1201 Peachtree Street NE
400 Colony Square, Suite 2100
Atlanta, GA 30361
Website: https://symptoms.webmd.com/default.htm#introView
Facebook and Twitter: @WebMD
This website allows people to check their symptoms when they're
worried that a sneeze, cough, or round of vomiting could be
something more serious.

FOR FURTHER READING

Asselin, Kristine Curtis, and Mitchell Walkowicz, ed. *Dangerous Diseases: Scary Illnesses that Frighten the World*. Mankato, MN: Capstone Press, 2014.

Cline-Ransome, Lesa, and James Ransome. *Germs: Fact and Fiction, Friends and Foes*. New York, NY: Henry Holt and Co., 2017.

Cohen, Robert. *Let's Find Out! The Stomach and Intestines in Your Body*. New York, NY: Rosen Publishing, 2015.

Farrell, Jeanette. *Invisible Enemies, Revised Edition: Stories of Infectious Disease*. New York, NY: Farrar, Strauss, and Giroux, 2005.

Figorito, Christine. *Let's Find Out! The Lungs in Your Body*. New York, NY: Rosen Publishing, 2015.

Murphy, Jim. *Invincible Microbe: Tuberculosis and the Never-Ending Search for a Cure*. New York, NY: HMH for Younger Readers, 2015.

Ollhoff, Jim. *A History of Germs: The Flu*. Mankato, MN: ABDO & Daughters, 2009.

Ollhoff, Jim. *A History of Germs: Smallpox*. Mankato, MN: ABDO & Daughters, 2009.

Strange, Christopher. *The Guide for Curious Minds: The Brain Explained*, New York, NY: Rosen Publishing, 2014.

White, Linda B., Barbara H. Seeber, and Barbara Brownell Grogan. *The Little Book of Home Remedies, Aches and Ailments: Natural Recipes to Ease Common Ailments*. Beverly, MA: Fair Winds Press, 2015.

BIBLIOGRAPHY

Aronson, Stanley M., MD. "The Origins of the Sneeze: Divine Gift or Mere Goldenrod Pollen?" *Rhode Island Medical Journal,* May 1, 2014, pp. 10–11.

Barth, Amy. "Sneeze Scientist." *Science World*, February 13, 2017, pp. 18–19.

Bhutta, Mahmood. "Sneezing Induced by Bladder Fullness." *International Journal of Urology*, February 2015, pp. 239.

Bowen, Richard. "Physiology of Vomiting." Vivi.colostate.edu. Retrieved October 4, 2017. http://www.vivo.colostate.edu/hbooks/pathphys /digestion/stomach/vomiting.html.

The Brain Made Simple. "Medulla Oblongata." Retrieved October 4, 2017. http://brainmadesimple.com/medulla-oblongata.html.

Calderone, Julia, and Skye Gould. "Here's What the Color of Your Snot Really Means." Business Insider, January 29, 2016. http://www.businessinsider.com /snot-color-green-yellow-sinus-infection-cold-2016-1/#-1.

Centers for Disease Control and Prevention. "Cold Versus Flu." CDC .gov, August 11, 2016. https://www.cdc.gov/flu/about/qa/coldflu.htm.

Current Health Kids. "You Asked…" December 2010, p. 23.

Dold, Kristen. "7 Possible Reasons Why You're Coughing." *Women's Health*, January 26, 2016. https://www.womenshealthmag.com /health/whats-causing-your-cough.

Gehl, Laura. "Ask Dr. Cy Borg." *Odyssey*, November/December 2014, pp. 44–45.

Ghayourmanesh, Soraya, PhD. "Sneezing." "Coughing." "Nausea and Vomiting." *Magill's Medical Guide (Online edition)*, January 2017.

Health Harvard Publishing. "That Nagging Cough." August 17, 2017. https://www.health.harvard.edu/staying-healthy/that-nagging-cough.

Hetzel, Megan. "5 Reasons That Running Can Make You Puke." *Runner's World*, November 29, 2016. https://www.runnersworld.com /health/5-reasons-that-running-can-make-you-puke.

Iwata, T., et al. "Mechanical Stimulation by Postnasal Drip Evokes Cough." *Plos One*, November 18, pp. 2–15.

Jurca, M., et al. "Prevalence of Cough Throughout Childhood: A Cohort Study." *Plos One*, May 24, 2017.

Mahashur, Ashok. "Chronic dry cough: Diagnostic and management approaches." *Lung India*, vol, 32 (1) Jan–Feb 2015. https://www.ncbi.nlm.nih.gov/pmc/articles/PMC4298918/.

Mayo Clinic. "Nausea and Vomiting." June 16, 2017. http://www.mayoclinic.org/symptoms/nausea/basics/definition/sym-20050736.

Miller, Brian Joseph. "What is Vomiting?" Everyday Health.com, April 24, 2017. https://www.everydayhealth.com/vomiting/guide.

Moore, Kristeen. "Whooping Cough (Pertussis)." Healthline.com, December 18, 2015. https://www.healthline.com/health/pertussis#overview1.

National Health Service. "Nausea and Vomiting in Adults." NHS.uk, December 19, 2016. http://www.nhs.uk/conditions/vomiting-adults/Pages/Introduction.aspx.

New York Times. "Asthma: In-Depth Report." June 23, 2013. http://www.nytimes.com/health/guides/disease/asthma/in-depth-report.html.

New York Times. "Cough." *New York Times Health Guide*, May 25, 2011. http://www.nytimes.com/health/guides/symptoms/cough/overview.html?mcubz=1.

New York Times. "Nausea and Vomiting—Adults." *New York Times Health Guide*, November 9, 2011. http://www.nytimes.com/health/guides/symptoms/nausea-and-vomiting/overview.html.

Nordqvist, Christian. "Coughs: Causes, Symptoms, and Treatments." *Medical News Today*, December 6, 2016. https://www.medicalnewstoday.com/articles/220349.php.

Satia, Imran, et al. "Towards Understanding and Managing Chronic Cough." *Clinical Medicine*. December 2016. https://www.researchgate.net/publication/312235127_Towards_understanding_and_managing_chronic_cough.

Science World. "You Asked…" February 22, 1999, p. 22.

Today's Parent. "Ultimate Guide to Kid Vomit: Causes and Treatment." October 26, 2016. https://www.todaysparent.com/kids/kids-health /ultimate-guide-to-kid-puke.

University of Washington. "Regulation of Emesis." Washington.edu. Retrieved October 4, 2017. https://courses.washington.edu/conj /bess/emesis/emesis.html.

Watson, Stephanie. "The Truth About Mucus." WebMD.com, April 10, 2014. https://www.webmd.com/allergies/features /the-truth-about-mucus?print=true.

WebMD.com. "Dry Coughs." WebMD.com. Retrieved October 4, 2017. https://www.webmd.com/cold-and-flu/tc /dry-coughs-topic-overview.

WebMD. "Nausea and Vomiting." Retrieved October 4, 2017. https:// www.webmd.com/digestive-disorders /digestive-diseases-nausea-vomiting#1.

WebMD. "Nausea and Vomiting and Thick Saliva or Mucus." Symptomcheckerwebmd.com. Retrieved October 4, 2017. http:// symptomchecker.webmd.com/multiple-symptoms ?symptoms=nausea-or-vomiting%7Cthick-saliva-or-mucus &symptomids=156%7C233&locations=22%7C7.

Whelan, Corey. "Can You Cough So Hard That You Vomit?" Healthline .com, March 16, 2017. https://www.healthline.com/health /can-you-cough-so-hard-that-you-vomit#overview1.

Wooten, Anne, and Michelle Bryner. "FYI." *Popular Science*, December 2007, pp. 131–134.

INDEX

ABOUT THE AUTHOR

Rachel Gluckstern is a writer and editor living in New York City. Her specialties range from education to religion and pop culture, and now, super gross science.

PHOTO CREDITS

Cover William Radcliffe/Science Faction/Getty Images; cover, pp. 7, 14, 20, 27, 33 (background) Chiari VFX/Shutterstock.com; pp. 1, 4–5 (background) matthew25/Shutterstock.com; p. 5 © iStockphoto .com/cglade; p. 8 Krieng Meemano/Shutterstock.com; p. 9 © iStockphoto.com/Catalin205; p. 12 Prostock-studio/Shutterstock.com; p. 15 Photon Illustration/Stocktrek Images/Getty Images; p. 18 Africa Studio/Shutterstock.com; p. 21 Daisy-Daisy/iStock/Thinkstock; p. 23 Ian Cuming/Ikon Images/Getty Images; p. 25 © iStockphoto.com/Leo Patrizi; p. 28 © iStockphoto.com/fstop123; p. 29 © iStockphoto.com/Mehmet Hilmi Barcin; p. 31 leungchopan/Shutterstock.com; p. 33 Stockbyte/ Thinkstock; p. 35 Nicoleta Ionescu/Shutterstock.com; p 37 © iStockphoto.com/princessdlaf.

Design: Michael Moy; Editor: Bethany Bryan; Photo Researcher: Sherri Jackson